# HEAD NORTH

## FINDING HAPPINESS THROUGH TRUE WEALTH

BY KEVIN ENGBERS, CFP®

It is important to have a proactive game plan for
your financial & life goals. It should be inspired
& designed on your core values, passions & purpose.
Its not what you make but what you do with
what you make that often is the difference. Have a plan!
then Confidently ENJOY Life!

# HEAD NORTH

## FINDING HAPPINESS THROUGH TRUE WEALTH

BY KEVIN ENGBERS, CFP®

THRONE
PUBLISHING GROUP

Throne Publishing Group
2329 N. Career Ave. #215
Sioux Falls, SD 57107
ThronePG.com

# ACKNOWLEDGMENTS

*This book is dedicated to:*

Linda, my soul mate on this journey called life; our four sons; daughters by marriage; and grandchildren, who inspire and motivate me.

Mom, for her strength and courage even through loss.

Dad—I miss you, our talks, and your wisdom.

*Personal thank-you:*

Happiness Resort

Dave and Cindy Ferris

4609 Happiness LN NW

Hackensack, MN 56452

*Professional thank-you:*

Throne Publishing, Sioux Falls; Peak Advisor Alliance, Omaha; and The True Wealth Institute, Omaha

*Authors:*

Steven Sanduski, MPA, CFP®

Ron Carson, CFP®, CFS, ChfC®

*Avalanche*—A Modern Parable

The Nine Principles of Uncovering True Wealth

# TABLE OF CONTENTS

*Introduction: Finding Happiness in True Wealth*      *xi*

**1  The Road to Happiness**      **1**

Looking for Happiness in All
   the Wrong Places      3

The Road North      7

True Happiness      10

A Road Map for Happiness      13


**2  Live a Life of Love**      **17**

Can't Buy Me Love      19

The Power of Love      22

What the World Needs Is Love, Sweet Love      24

The Book of Love      26

**3  Stick to Your Core Values**                          **29**

Hitting Dead Ends                                          31

Setting Your Compass                                       33

Following Your Heart                                       35

H.E.A.R.T.                                                 36

Mapping Out Your Values                                    39


**4  Be Purpose Driven**                                  **43**

The Ultimate Question                                      45

Detours Can Pave the Way                                   50

Heading in the Right Direction                             54

Charting Your Course                                       55


**5  Be Accountable Through Your Goals**                  **59**

Setting Goals for the Wrong Reasons                        61

Aligning Goals                                             64

The Driving Force of Goals                                 65

Reaching Our Mileposts                                     67


**6  Cherish Relationships**                              **71**

Where Meaning is Found                                     73

Before it's Too Late   76

What it Means to Cherish   78

Creating a Ripple Effect   80

**7   Value Your Health   83**

The Cost of Running Out of Gas   85

The Balance Between Survival and Excess   88

Where All Roads Converge   91

Driving a Well-Oiled Machine   93

**8   Wisely Use Your Financial Resources   97**

Veering Off Course   99

Striking a Balance   102

Deepening Your Relationship with Money   103

How to Instill Confidence about Money   105

**9   Be Compassionate with the World   111**

Giving Until it Feels Good   113

True Compassion   117

Sharing Our True Wealth with Others   119

Finding the Passion in Compassion   120

**10 Be Open to Wise Counselors**     **123**

Learning from Our Experiences     125

Unexpected Counselors     128

What it Means to be Wise     129

Learning from Others     131

*Conclusion: Finding Your Road North*     *135*

*Bibliography*     *139*

*About the Author*     *143*

# INTRODUCTION: FINDING HAPPINESS IN TRUE WEALTH

*"Happiness is the meaning and the purpose of life, the whole aim and end of human existence."*
—Aristotle

We live in an affluent society in which most of us have the means, but unfortunately, not all of us have the meaning. Money does not buy meaning. Of course, the desire to strive for a secure financial future is natural, but more important is finding the right balance and uncovering a deeper meaning in life.

The financial industry often focuses on the building of wealth and looking into the future. Although we incorporate most of those principles, our overall approach is refreshingly different. If we helped you retire but you were not able to enjoy the journey along the way to the end of your life, we did not fulfill our passion and personal mission. Our financial purpose is much bigger than that—it's a life purpose, not a retirement purpose.

As a Certified Financial Planner™ Practitioner and wealth advisor, it's my purpose to strive to take you to a higher pinnacle of wealth that I call "True Wealth."

I've seen these principles lived out, especially in my dad's life, and I know they work. What's great about them is that they serve as a road map for you to come back to and judge whether you are heading in the right direction. In deciding to share with you the road north—*and what it means*—I have to admit this journey is as much a self-help guide for me as I hope it can be a learning experience for you. I don't profess to have mastered every aspect of True Wealth; I'm not pursuing perfection but instead a perfect effort.

Many people struggle financially because of a wrong focus. Life is not only about the money; there's so much more to living than earning a living.

Wealth goes beyond financial concerns. The question you should be asking is, "Am I improving the situations of those I love and the world around me?" Remember, if you feel you're in a rat race, even if you win, you're still a rat.

Understanding the principles in this book will be freeing and should help you live a more satisfying life by helping you refocus on what's truly important. Oftentimes, people focus on the money and lose sight of the other things, and if you focus only on the other things you find important, you'll find you can't fulfill them without having money. By striking an appropriate balance, you can find happiness and still afford to lead a more fulfilling life. This book is a philosophy, an approach to finding that.

My goal is to help you create a road map that will guide you in your journey toward happiness—which can be found in True Wealth—so you can connect your meaning to your money and your life. My other goals for writing this book are to

- point you in a direction so you have no regrets at the end of your life, because you strove to live a life that was aligned and balanced;
- inspire you to enjoy the view from where you are instead of saying "Now what?"; and
- help you gain better clarity about where you are, where you're headed, and whether you need to change roads and to show you how to identify which roads might lead you to a more fulfilling life.

## Chapter 1

# THE ROAD
# TO HAPPINESS

*"If you don't know where you are going,*
*any road will get you there."*

—Lewis Carroll

## LOOKING FOR HAPPINESS
## IN ALL THE WRONG PLACES

As a financial planner, I often talk with people about the "road to retirement." This includes all the detours and obstacles that may reroute them and the potential opportunities to help them stay focused on the journey. What I've realized after many years in the financial field is that life is not just about the road to retirement; it's about the "road to *happiness.*" Happiness is a journey, and my responsibility as a financial adviser is that of a cartographer to help map out the roads you might consider taking, the ones that might lead you to happiness. The problem is that many of us think there's only one road that leads to happiness—money.

According to Richard Layard in his book *Happiness*, people's average income has more than doubled over the past fifty years, yet on average, people are no happier today than when Elvis appeared on the *Ed Sullivan Show* in 1957. In working with people, I am fascinated by how money affects them. A friend who inherited a significant amount of money once told me, "I used to worry about not having enough money, and now that I have more money than I will ever need, I sleep even less at night." I've worked with scores of people over the years and can attest that the happiest people are not always the wealthiest. If money is your final destination, you'll often end up frustrated.

It's not at all uncommon to want material possessions, believing they'll make you happy. To some extent, they do, at least for a period of time. What tends to happen, though, is we get stuck on what researchers call the "hedonic treadmill." We quickly get used to these new things, and they become part of our norm. For example, once we get more financial resources, we become accustomed to having more and want to find the next thing that will take our level of happiness up a notch. We end up constantly striving and never arriving.

I still chuckle remembering a conversation I had with someone regarding taxes. The current mantra among many in the country is that it's time to start taxing the rich, that top 1 percent who by some definitions have been getting by without paying their fair share. In this conversation, we were discussing the wisdom of this idea, and he quipped, "All I know it is high time we start taxing the rich." Because I was this person's adviser and had an understanding of his net worth, I asked him, "You realize you are probably talking about yourself, right?" He responded, "I'm not rich." I was a bit confused, so I asked him to clarify. "You have several million dollars. If you're not rich, then who is?" He responded, "Anyone with a dollar more than me."

The saddest part of this story is that if he had maintained that mindset, he could have struggled to achieve True Wealth or know true happiness because there would always be someone who had one more dollar than he had. Not only was his destination off course, but the road he was choosing would never have led him there. Now, one area that has puzzled me over the years is the financial term "wealth." If you have accumulated 500, 5,000, or 500,000 dollars, it represents your wealth. However, most of us tend to believe that wealth is a specific, higher level of having certain things. The client relationships I build elevate the emphasis on *having things* to *doing* and *being*. Looking at this concept of doing and being in greater detail can help you find your own road to happiness. In reality, there are many roads to happiness; you just need to know where you're headed to determine whether you're on the right one.

An ad I came across put it well: roads can take you anywhere—to the boathouse, the beach house, or even the poorhouse. There's a famous scene in Lewis

Carroll's *Alice in Wonderland* where Alice comes to a fork in the road. As she's contemplating her options, she sees the Cheshire Cat, whom she asks, "Would you tell me, please, which way I ought to go from here?"

"That depends a good deal on where you want to get to," said the Cat.

"I don't much care where—," started Alice.

"Then it doesn't much matter which way you go."

We smile at this exchange, but it raises an important question. *Do you know where you are, where you want to go, and whether the road you're on will take you there?*

## THE ROAD NORTH

The road north is one of my favorites. There are several roads I have taken north, each one paved with traditions, memories, and new adventures, but the destination remains the same—*Happiness*. The road north has come to symbolize my own journey to happiness in life. For fifty-five of fifty-six years of my life, our family has spent the last week of July and the first week of August "finding happiness." We missed the road north only once in my life. That was the year my wife and I were awaiting the birth of our third son. I like to joke how I couldn't believe we hadn't done better planning the previous year, but the year's hiatus delivered another member of the family who would soon learn what it means to discover happiness.

Last year, as I enjoyed the hum of the car tires on the road north, I found myself reflecting on the journeys to happiness. I was sure I heard a small voice from the backseat. The words were so familiar—words I had whispered as a small boy, words echoed by each of my children: "Dad. Hey, Dad ... are we there yet?"

Like that of the father before me came the response, "Where's that, son?"

"Happiness!" as if there were anywhere else we could be going.

"Not yet, but we're closer than when we started."

Paul Bunyan's sweetheart, Lucette Diana Kensack, was said to have called this region up north home. Nestled on the edge of the Chippewa National Forest is 24.8 miles of shoreline that surrounds the

5,080 acres of water we affectionately call "the Lake." Boasting twenty-two-foot clarity with depths over two hundred feet, the Lake showcases a resort called Happiness.

There's a simplicity about Happiness. It could be a competitive card game of Peanuts or Hearts; having a cup of joe with my son, Jon, at sunrise; a variety of games on the beach; a head-over-heels tube ride; or S'mores at sunset and the crackle of a campfire. It's a time when I don't have to worry about things. It's not luxurious or expensive; it's time spent with real people. It's totally achievable and within reach. It's about the relationships that are there, the memories created, and making a priority of carving out time with the people important to me. It's a place—and it's not a place. This is my physical representation of True Wealth—those things money can't buy and death can't take away.

It took "Taps" and the echoes of the twenty-one-gun salute at my dad's funeral to remind me of how he had embraced the concepts of True Wealth. He had provided me with an example of how to try to live it.

Dad was one of the happiest, most content men I knew. His passing gave a lot of these things new meaning. I have attended the True Wealth Institute in Omaha, read many self-help books, and been trying to teach the concepts and principles of True Wealth for many years, but Dad tried to live them. My hope is that it doesn't take something like this for you to discover what truly makes you happy. You need to find your own happiness, your own True Wealth. Just like my dad, you won't always get every aspect right, but you and those around you are better when you try. So how exactly do you do that?

## TRUE HAPPINESS

Lexus advertised one of its models with the caption, "Whoever said money can't buy happiness isn't spending it right." It's certainly clever and appeals to your desire to appear successful but goes against what research tells us about what really makes people happy. Happiness isn't determined by our external circumstances or how much money's in our bank accounts, as many of us believe.

According to Dr. Emiliana Simon-Thomas of the Greater Good Science Center at the University of California in Berkeley,

> "Researchers think of happiness as having satisfaction and meaning in your life. It's the propensity to feel positive emotions, the capacity to recover from negative emotions quickly, and holding a sense of purpose. Happiness is not having a lot of privilege or money. It's not constant pleasure. It's a broader thing: our ability to connect with others, to have meaningful relationships, to have a community. Time and again—across decades of research and across all studies—people who say they're happy have strong connections with community and with other people. That's sort of the recipe for happiness." ("What Is the Science of Happiness?" 2015)

I couldn't agree more. So how do we attain this sort of happiness? Start by realizing it's more than just money. Redefine your definition of wealth. Picture what your life would look like if you were financially confident, physically fit, spiritually nourished, purpose driven, intellectually engaged, and surrounded by loving relationships. What would your life look like? Chances are when you have this kind of life, you're filled with energy and enthusiasm. You greet each day with gratefulness and a smile. You walk around lighter than air, trying to bring joy to everyone you meet. You strive to make a positive difference in your relationships, your neighborhood, and your community.

Do you want this kind of life? Sure, we all do, and I'm writing this book because it's available to you. This is True Wealth. It resides at the intersection of physical, spiritual, emotional, and financial health. Aligning these areas in your life can lead to enjoying life's great moments. Happiness is the reward of a life in balance. When you set a course for True Wealth, you set yourself up for a happier, more fulfilling life.

Happiness is a journey. Knowing which road you're on can make a difference. Are you choosing roads of positive emotion or constant worry? Do your roads lead to gratitude for what you have or down a dead end of never having enough? Are you headed for the crossroads of physical, spiritual, emotional, and financial health, or is your course set on the one-way road of possible financial gain? It's important to enjoy the journey and all the bumps and detours along the way, but it's equally important to know where you're going and have a road map for how to get there. Your positive emotions and perceptions can help you navigate the detours, and the principles of True Wealth provide the road map.

## A ROAD MAP FOR HAPPINESS

When it comes to happiness, even Abraham Lincoln had something to say: "People are just about as happy as they make up their minds to be." We're learning that, as our emotions ebb and flow, so do our brain chemistry and blood flow. Fear, depression, and love all get different parts of our brains working. Positive emotions, such as happiness, enthusiasm, and joy, show as increased activity on the left side of the brain. This means the more often we choose positive emotions, such as gratitude, love, and laughter, the more our bodies will produce positive effects in our brains and lead to more feelings of happiness.

Think about what makes you happy. Is it spending time with loved ones? Visiting a special place? Enjoying a home-cooked meal? Write down the things that make you happy. Next to each one, write down the date you last experienced it. Do you have anything on your list that you haven't experienced in the past twenty-four hours? How about the past twenty-four days? The past twenty-four months? Twenty-four years? If your list isn't as up to date as you'd like it to be, here are a few things that researchers say can make you happier:

1.  Count your blessings. Studies have shown that being grateful has numerous benefits, including helping you feel better about your life. You'll be more optimistic about your future; improve your health; feel more joyful, enthusiastic, and energetic; and even get more sleep at night. People who are habitually

grateful have also been shown to more frequently engage in kind or helpful behaviors. And, finally, being grateful has been known to make hair grow back. (Well, not really, but I made you stop and think.)

2. Savor life's joys. Taking the time to notice life's simple beauty can make you happier. One of the best ways to do this is to try to see the world through the eyes of a child, where everything is new. Regaining that attitude can help you appreciate the beauty around you.

3. Develop strategies for coping with stress and hardships. You can rely on faith. Some people may turn to exercise. Or how about this one—learn to laugh more. I'm serious. Laughing will bring positive emotion into your body, which can help you heal quicker.

As a financial adviser, one of my passions is to discover what brings happiness into people's lives and see how I can try to bring more of it more often. This is where the nine principles of True Wealth come in and what the rest of this book is dedicated to. By trying to live these nine principles, my hope is that you'll experience greater happiness and leave this world a much better place than when you arrived. So let's get started.

## Chapter 2

# LIVE A LIFE OF LOVE

*"Love is the essential fact. It is our ultimate reality and our purpose on earth. To be consciously aware of it, to experience love in ourselves and others, is the meaning of life."*

—Marianne Williamson

## CAN'T BUY ME LOVE

If there's one thing we all want more of in our lives, it's love. This may sound a little cheesy, but it's true. We want the love of our parents, our children, our spouse, our friends. Just think about all the songs that have been written about love. The Beatles told us that "All You Need Is Love." Elvis pleaded to "Love Me Tender." Andy Williams told us about the "Love Story." Celine Dion sang about "The Power of Love," and Jackie DeShannon told us that "What the World Needs Now Is Love, Sweet Love." And here's my favorite, "I Think I Love You" by the Partridge Family.

When I was growing up as a pastor's kid, scripture played an important role in my life. I learned a lot about love from verses many of us are familiar with, such as 1 Corinthians 13:4–8: "Love is patient, love is kind. It does not envy, it does not boast, it is not proud, it is not rude, not self-seeking, not easily angered. Love does not delight in evil but rejoices with the truth. It always protects, always trusts, always hopes, always endures. Love never fails."

Although it's difficult to admit, for a long time I believed I understood what a life of love meant, but my idea was backward. It was the world's version of love, which is conditional, convenient, and self-serving.

I thought all these things were what I was supposed to *get* from love, but that's not how it works. Love isn't about how much we *get*; it's about how much we *give*. It isn't as the world teaches: I will love you if I get something in return, when I need something, or if you love me. It becomes confusing when certain activist groups remind us that they believe in love and we are to accept them out of love. Then they carry out threats or acts of intolerance, which is not what the first True Wealth principle of living a life of love is trying to encourage. The verses remind me of what we are being called to do regardless of whether we receive the same back from someone else. It's certainly not always easy on the road to happiness—especially when someone cuts in front of you in traffic.

Another misconception many of us have is we think money can buy us love. This is just another way of trying to get what we're looking for. We look to possessions and other material things to fill the void we feel. We all have this yearning, but how many of us are taking the first steps necessary to have more love in our lives? How many of us are being a living example of love? How many of us are responding to the situations in our lives with a loving heart?

## THE POWER OF LOVE

One of the greatest ways my dad taught me about the principle of love was by giving of his time. Verbal I love you and hugs are not often found from conservative men of Dutch heritage. I'm fortunate to have experienced both expressions before he passed, but throughout my life I never questioned his love, even when he disciplined me.

The road north is so special to me. As a minister, my dad was very busy. In church, the man in the pulpit was my pastor, but when he set aside time for me—one of life's most precious commodities—the road north and a red Lund fishing boat allowed me to learn to tie a fishing knot from my hero—Dad. My dad taught me about the fruits of the Spirit—love, gentleness, kindness—by what he did to *be* love. In 2016, my happiness would be tested, but as I expected, it did not break. For the first time in over fifty-six years, my dad—known as Big Grandpa by some and the Emperor of the Lake by local residents and guests—was physically not with me. The crappies of Ten Mile now swim fearlessly, for the little red Lund has a younger, less experienced pilot.

My dad knew he was here for two purposes: to be a fisherman and a fisher of men. I would often hear him say, "When I leave this world, I hope I'm either behind a pulpit or in my red Lund." He seemed to know how to balance his life to be both these things and do them well. He was here to give to others as much as he was here to catch his fish. It was easy for him to be in a position of servitude; he found as much joy serving as he did preaching from the pulpit, which left a lasting impression on me. Even though he was a busy man, he made time for everyone. Now that he's gone, I often reflect on how many years I spent working more than being home with my sons. I was in a catch-22: when I was at work, all I could think about was being home; when I was home, all I could think about was the need to be at work. Not only did my dad make time for his family; he would also visit and care for the sick and elderly. Seeing him do this, I experienced what love truly meant. He taught me it was something we have to reach out to do, not just something we receive.

## WHAT THE WORLD NEEDS
## IS LOVE, SWEET LOVE

Living a life of love means living a life of service and being kind to others, as expressed in 1 John 3:16–17: "This is how we know what love is: Jesus Christ laid down his life for us. And we ought to lay down our lives for our brothers. If anyone has material possessions and sees his brother in need but has no pity on him, how can the love of God be in him? Let us not love with words or tongue but with actions and in truth."

It does require you to change the direction of love from what you get to what you give. How many of us have counted how many good friends we have? How many of us check our social media accounts to see how many new friends we have or how people reacted to our latest post? What we might ask instead is, how many people have I been a good friend to? How many people have I engaged with—online and offline? I first have to *be* a good friend before I can *have* a good friend.

Love is the first principle of True Wealth because it is the foundation on which we live and give. Having a heart of love means giving with no strings attached. The focus shifts from how much is accumulated to how much is given. Money can be a tool to show love. There are plenty of opportunities around the world and even down the street to use your resources to show love to others. There's a fine line to walk here. Some people buy into the "prosperity gospel," which teaches "give and you will be blessed," when really you should give because you *have* been blessed. When you give, you *are* blessed. True giving comes from a heart of love, and the motive is what really matters. It's not always an easy thing to give and not expect anything in return. In the back of your mind, you might think, *I hope I didn't give away my last meal.* But what I've learned is that if my heart is right, everything else falls into place. Your motive to give should be the same as why you live.

Giving out of love leads to greater happiness, which is why it's foundational to True Wealth. This might be in the form of money, time, patience, or a response to someone. In a seventy-five-year study, Harvard psychiatrist George Vaillant found that being patient with others and having close friends and a warm personality can lead to greater success (McKay and McKay 2014). He discovered that love is the key to a happy and fulfilling life. As Vaillant put it, "Happiness is only the cart; love is the horse" (Gregoire 2013).

## THE BOOK OF LOVE

It doesn't necessarily come naturally to give love in these ways, and it doesn't help that life is getting more complex. There are so many distractions. Living a life of love is a choice and something you commit to. You might stop and ask yourself, *What is my destination, and is the road I'm on going to get me there?* Does your road lead to time spent with the people who are most important in your life? Is it leading you to be a good friend? Is it leading you to be fully present with those you're with? Is it leading you to be of service in the world with what you can give? If it's not, it might be time to change course. If living a life of love is your destination, here are a few ways to get there:

1.  Be of service to others. Have you ever noticed how helping someone makes you feel better, even if it's as simple as holding a door open for an elderly person? Mahatma Gandhi said, "The best way to find yourself is to lose yourself in the service of others." When you act from a place of servitude, you put to use the fruits of the Spirit and bring joy to others and yourself.

2.  Learn to forgive. I could write a whole book on forgiveness, but for now, what I want you to think about is forgiving: let go of the anger, bitterness, and resentment. Anger and bitterness are destructive emotions that not only make you unhappy; they make you unhealthy. Dr. Fred Luskin of the Stanford University Forgiveness Project has found that forgiveness is a huge predictor of happiness.

If you're holding on to anger or resentment, you're keeping yourself from feeling fulfilled (Nuff 2014).

3. Look in the mirror each morning and ask yourself, *Do I like the person looking back at me?* Living a life of love means starting with yourself. You can't give what you don't have. By filling up your own tank and learning to feel worthy of love, you can more easily give love to others.

The more you can live your life with a loving spirit, the more you'll be able to transform yourself and the world around you into a joyful and happy place. Several cities, both nationally and internationally, have experienced recent acts of terror, and love and the Spirit's fruit appear absent. The world does need more "love, sweet love," but it starts with the person in the mirror. From here, the next stop is to explore what core values are guiding you on your road to happiness.

Chapter 3

# STICK TO YOUR
# CORE VALUES

*"Values provide perspective in the best
of times and the worst of times."*
—Charles Garfield

## HITTING DEAD ENDS

Life can sometimes feel like we're driving around in circles, not really getting anywhere. Far too many people go through life without enthusiasm. Many people spend their lives getting up, eating breakfast, going to work, putting out fires all day, coming home, eating dinner, trying to spend time with the kids, falling into bed, and starting all over the next day. You can do this your whole life and, in the end, not be fulfilled.

People struggle with finding true happiness because the things they do are incongruent with their values. By knowing your core values and sticking to them, you have a better idea of how to get where you want to go and to make the difficult times more manageable. Defining what's important to you is the foundation to living a happier life.

Values are principles that you believe in—the things you go to right away when you need to make a decision. They are your center, your innermost beliefs, and what you use to determine how you're going to conduct yourself. They help you decide right from wrong with clarity and focus. But many people don't consciously think about what their values are. I'm not talking about material things, such as your car or boat. I'm talking about things such as your family, your health, your reputation, your spiritual life, and your legacy. Perhaps it's being a good steward of the financial resources that have been entrusted to you or having the belief that family is of fundamental importance. You might live by "honesty is always the best policy" or "trust has to be earned." Or perhaps one of your values is seeing the importance of a healthy work–life balance. Whatever your values might be, locating them on your compass and moving toward them on your road to happiness is important in the second True Wealth principle: stick to your core values.

## SETTING YOUR COMPASS

Some of my best fishing conversations with Dad were about the importance of having good values and principles and their being true north on my compass. Dad didn't teach me by lecturing or preaching—even though he spoke from the pulpit with great passion. I could *see* his values through his actions. Although it's something he tried to do throughout the year, he wanted to make sure he protected his core value of family by ensuring we spent time together. For more than fifty years, he made it a priority to set time aside and take the road north for happiness.

To this day, I can be in a neutral location, and a certain smell, caw of a crow, call of the loon, or even a slamming wooden screen door will instantly transport me to where my family found happiness. One of my favorite side excursions was when we went to different lakes to fish. We'd get up early, have a hearty breakfast at the local café, and then head off for the day's adventure. One of my favorite places was a very secluded lake, Lake Stewart. There were only two cabins on the lake, and although it wasn't far from where we were and was roughly two miles off the main road, it took us three hours to get there in the most rustic off-road vehicle imaginable. I remember thinking we were headed to a place from which no person returned. But we knew where we were going; we'd taken the necessary steps to adequately prepare for anything. We'd packed food, clothing for any change in weather, and a generator. After all, there was no electricity, and we were being dropped off for several hours. Because we'd planned for the expected and prepared for the unexpected, we were able to relax and savor the time away. I don't remember whether there was even a way to contact anyone outside of the Lake Stewart area, because this was a time before cell phones and we would've certainly been outside any coverage area. Even today, the cell phone reception at the end of our road north requires a certain body contortion at the end of the dock. Looking back, I recall the fishing was very good, but it was our challenges along the journey that provided the most memorable experiences.

The experiences you have with the people who are most important to you often bring a deeper fulfillment. Life's not always paved with straight, smooth surfaces. There're times you will encounter potholes and obstacles, but when you know what's important to you and your compass is properly calibrated, life is good. You can live out your core values anywhere. For us, it just happened to be on a lake at the end of the road north. After seeing my dad calibrate his core values, I felt how important it was to discover my own.

## FOLLOWING YOUR HEART

One of the exercises we take people through in the Five Blueprinting Steps to True Wealth involves developing a compelling personal mission statement. In this process, we work through defining what's important to you, evaluating your core values with a meaningful purpose in an effort to develop a compelling mission statement, and living a life based on that. We try to get your compelling mission down to a three-word sentence or, if possible, one word. For me, the five blueprinting step process provided a one-word acronym: H.E.A.R.T. After all, the heart is where our core values live. I wanted to have something to point to when I hit a pothole or detour or came to a crossroad so I could immediately refocus by asking myself, *Does this align with my H.E.A.R.T.?*

## H.E.A.R.T.

H = Hear God's calling. I always want to know whether I'm doing the things I believe my Creator wants me to do. Even if you don't have a similar spirituality, it's important for you to discover what drives you.

E = Emulate Christ. I like to ask myself, *What would Christ do?* Even though I may fail most days at doing what He would do, there's still a beauty to having this checkpoint. I have something by which to measure myself time and time again to see whether my compass is still pointing to my true north.

A = Always be present. This certainly isn't an easy one. I've struggled in life, thinking I should be at work when I'm at home or I should be at home when I'm at work. I've found the key for me is that wherever I am, I do whatever I can to be *there.*

R = Relationships. This helps me check in and remember relationships. Am I developing meaningful relationships with people at work and at home? I talked about the importance of living a life of love, and this reminds me of one specific area that I've defined as important to me—relationships.

T = Trust. Do I have relationships that are deep enough to develop a level of trust? Maybe, more important, can I trust my own heart? If my heart is right, other things seem to fall into place.

When my H.E.A.R.T. isn't aligned with my actions I have a feeling of anger, trip up with the wrong language, or become less tolerant of others. If I can keep these core values front and center, I do better in the other areas of life. When I'm doing these things consistently, I'm happy. I know I'm heading in the right direction, and I have a sense of purpose. When I'm not following my heart, I'm not always happy with myself. It's important for me to have my compelling vision and mission represent the things that are important to me. I don't expect my H.E.A.R.T. will ever be perfect, but it is important to me to provide a perfect effort.

By knowing your values, you can consciously spend more time living them out. When you live your values, you are honoring yourself, and your life is better aligned with the things that are most important to you. The more time you can spend doing and living by the things most important to you, the happier you are going to be. Think back to a time when you were happiest in your life. Maybe it was a family vacation, a spiritual awakening, or the time you spent with someone close to you. I think you'll find that at those times, you were fully engaged in living out your core values.

Equally, by being clear on your core values, you can be a better decision maker. When presented with a fork in the road, you can always fall back on your core values and ask yourself, *What is truly important to me?* By knowing this, it's much easier to choose the road to take that is most in line with where you are being called to go.

Once you are clear on that, it will still take energy to get there. Focusing on your values can give you the motivation and energy you need. Dr. Jack Groppel, a noted exercise physiologist, says we have only two sources for energy—the physical and the spiritual. He defines spiritual as values. When you're focused on your values and engaged in activities that fit your capacity, you have the ability to make great achievements. Being clear on your values is the key that catalyzes achievement.

## MAPPING OUT YOUR VALUES

Having strong convictions about what you value helps you stay balanced and focused. This is different for each person and might change over time. It's important to define what's important to you and to make sure your life is in sync with that. Doing this isn't just a one-time event; it's a lifelong journey.

As a CERTIFIED FINANCIAL PLANNER™ practitioner and wealth adviser, I strive to incorporate all the traditional planning principles but broaden the approach to something refreshingly different. I like to think of my approach as that of a financial cartographer. I focus on how money and True Wealth intertwine with your values and map out potential strategies to assist you on your journey. To me, money is a tool you've been given to manage. How you manage it allows you to spend more time on what you define as important and to make a difference in other people's lives. When you manage your money in accordance with your core values, you can feel more confident. Money takes on a new meaning when you start to look at it this way. Here are a few ways to get clearer on just what your core values are:

1. Uncover your beliefs about money. We start with money because we often think that's what's important to us. Start by finishing the following

sentences: "Having more money would allow me to ..." and "Money is ..." Then, think or write about your earliest recollection of money. How you manage money and the importance you place on it was taught to you in either a conscious or subconscious way at a very young age. Did your parents talk about money, or was the subject taboo? Was it a source of anger or enjoyment? Understanding your money philosophies and core values potentially helps avoid relationship conflicts.

2. Define your True Wealth—all you have that money can't buy and death can't take away. List examples of these things in your life. Doing this will help point you to what you define as truly important.

3. Hone in on your values. Imagine you go to a doctor and she tells you that you have only two weeks to live. What would be the first thing you would do? This will reveal what you define as important. Then ask yourself what you would do if you had only twenty-four hours to live. This will help you quickly hone in on the things that are most important to you. What you define as important is the foundation on which you build.

People who have done great things—those who have had a life of achievement—were people who lived their lives so committed to their core values and with such conviction that they were willing to devote their lives to them and, in some cases, even sacrificing their lives for them. Fortunately, many of us won't have to do that, but the key is to feel so strongly about what you value that you're willing to take action to reach your destination. Having convictions about what you value and being committed to living those values every day will go a long way to unleash your burning desire—your purpose—to live out your core values.

Chapter 4

# BE PURPOSE DRIVEN

*"Find a purpose in life so big*
*it will challenge every capacity*
*to be at your best."*
—David O. McKay

## THE ULTIMATE QUESTION

Why are you here?

This might be one of the hardest questions to answer. I believe all of us are here for a reason and that reason is something greater than ourselves. Consider this quote from Oliver Wendell Holmes Sr.:

> "A few can touch the magic string,
> and noisy Fame is proud to win them;
> Alas for those who never sing,
> But die with all their music in them!"

I believe that all of us have God-given talents and gifts. Unfortunately, some people are going to take their talents and gifts to the grave, never letting them see the light of day. Not only is that a tragedy for you if that happens; it's also a tragedy for the world, because the world can be a much better place if we're all operating at full capacity.

Our purpose is what we feel called to do; it gives meaning to our lives. But it isn't always easy to uncover. Once you understand what is important to you, you can start thinking about your purpose. Your core values and purpose intertwine. I believe your core values are those distinguishing things that align you with your purpose. Think of it this way: if core values are the clarity (setting your compass), then purpose is the action (starting the car). Your purpose is how you carry out your core values.

In this quote, Eric Hoffer talks about "the one thing you ought to do": "The feeling of being hurried is not usually the result of living a full life and having no time. It is, on the contrary, born of a vague fear that you are wasting your life. When you do not do the one thing you ought to do, you have no time for anything else— we are the busiest people in the world."

This quote is similar to what Gary Keller writes about in his book on the importance of finding that "one thing"—that thing that matters most in your life. When you are not focused on that one thing—your purpose—you instead spend your days scurrying about and filling your time with "stuff" you hope will make up for your lack of living your purpose. That's why you'll often hear me say there's more to living than earning a living.

Many of us have it backward and think that once we've accumulated enough money, then we can live our purpose. But it isn't until you figure out why you're here that you'll be motivated to live your life and manage your financial resources accordingly. It's one thing to talk about accumulating money; it's another to talk about what you believe the purpose of that money is. Being able to connect your financial resources with your purpose is a challenge. Some of us have been taught to think that whoever has the most chips in the end wins, but we can't take them with us, so it's really about how we use those chips along the way.

While I was attending the True Wealth Institute, I met a gentleman who had accumulated a lot of money. My initial impression was that he had it all figured out, but the further we went through the Five Blueprinting Steps, the clearer it became that he was struggling with the same thing most people struggle with: What is my purpose? What am I supposed to be doing? I was surprised to hear him utter these familiar words: "There has to be more to life than this." As we dug deeper, we discovered what he really wanted to do was to make a difference in the lives of troubled teens. He said he had always wanted to purchase a fast-food franchise so he could hire troubled teens, mentor them, and

becoming a pastor. His journey had sudden changes that led him down roads he'd not planned to travel. Dad never went to high school or college; he started out as a carpenter. One day, someone said to him, "Of all the people who are in heaven, how many of them are there because of you being a guiding light for them?" It was a simple question he could not get out of his mind. The thought of uprooting his family and taking a different road seemed strange to many because he didn't have a college degree, but it didn't sound strange to Dad and Mom because, despite every roadblock they met, unexplainable doors were opened as they followed their calling. Dad took the college entrance exam and completed college and seminary on an accelerated timetable, even when everyone told him he couldn't do it.

Your purpose develops along the way, and discovering it is a process. I believe I have a good understanding of mine, but it's a personal thing. My purpose isn't your purpose; it's something unique to each of us and something we all have to discover. The only thing that was similar is that I believe my dad's purpose also started with "hearing God's calling." I remember Dad saying it was a good thing not everyone is called to the ministry. If everyone in the world were a preacher, to whom would he have been called to preach?

We all have a different purpose, and each purpose is a vital part of a greater community and society—the more diverse, the more complete our society on this incredible journey called life.

## HEADING IN THE RIGHT DIRECTION

When you live your life both on purpose and with purpose, life flows. You're living the way you're called to live. You're making the contributions you're supposed to make. You're able to experience an unexplainable peace, and life is good. It doesn't get much better than that. Your purpose doesn't have to be an earth-shattering cure for cancer or an answer to world peace. It could be something far less glamorous but not less significant.

Although ultimate purpose stays the same, it looks a little different at different phases of our lives. Each step is necessary to get us to the next. I started out owning a clothing store, went into newspaper advertising, and ultimately became a financial planner and wealth adviser.

To me, meaningful purpose transcends what we do for ourselves and reaches out to the world around us and infuses all life with the special gifts each of us have. Some of them we are born with, such as natural talent, and some we pick up along the way, such as financial resources. The important thing is to look at how you use those gifts to carry out your purpose and make a difference in other people's lives. So let me be direct: Are you living your life's purpose?

## CHARTING YOUR COURSE

If you're having trouble thinking about what your meaningful purpose is, try writing your eulogy. Whoa, right? This was the most difficult exercise I was asked to complete while going through the course at the True Wealth Institute.

As Wayne Dyer said, "Death is experienced only once, but if you fear it, you will die in every minute of your life." Coming to grips with the fact that we're all going to die someday is an important issue to face head-on. One individual put things in perspective for me. Although I had not known him in a business relationship, I was visiting him near the end of his life. We'd talked about a lot of things when the conversation changed and he reflected on his life. He had a significant amount of financial resources. He told me, "Life is really interesting. When I was born, I came into this world in an eight-by-ten room. Now I find myself at the end of my life, I've amassed a lot of wealth, and here I am back in an eight-by-ten room." His main concern was, "Did I do it right? Did I do everything I could to make a difference?" Let's not get to the end to ask this question. Let's ask this question now so we can lead more meaningful lives and do what we're here to do. Here are a few ways to get clearer on your purpose and lead a more meaningful life:

1. Write your eulogy. This certainly isn't easy, but it helps you refocus on your purpose. Even starting this process can ground you really quickly.

Ask yourself, "What will people remember about me a hundred years from now? What lasting legacy will I leave?" Your material goods will be long gone and what remains will be the lives of the people you've touched—your family, your descendants, and other people with whom you have shared your generosity. So think about that. What can you do in the rest of your life that will still be positively remembered a hundred years from now?

2. Identify your gifts. Ask yourself, *Do I have any unique gifts? What are the things I do extremely well?* Then ask yourself whether you can use your talents or gifts to better society in some way. Looking at the intersection of your talents (either money or abilities) and what it is you're passionate about is likely where you'll find meaning and purpose.

3. Verify your life's purpose. If you can find the one thing that allows you to answer yes to the following five questions, then there's a good chance you've found it. Is it in your eulogy? Does it fulfill you? Does it feed a hunger (not only what you hunger for but also what the world hungers for)? Does it ignite passion? Is it compatible with your values?

Writing your eulogy is a great way to look back on your life and figure out, while you still have the time, what it is you want to do that will have a lasting effect. You know you have your eulogy just right when reading it gets you all choked up. Don't be bashful. Nobody has to read this eulogy right now except you. Dream a little. Stretch a little. Look deep inside and ask yourself, *What am I really here to do? What do I want to accomplish that will give my life significance?* This is how you get your compass calibrated to your true north.

## Chapter 5

# BE ACCOUNTABLE
# THROUGH YOUR
# GOALS

*"If you want to be happy, set a goal that commands your thoughts, liberates your energy and inspires your hopes."*

—Andrew Carnegie

## SETTING GOALS FOR THE WRONG REASONS

Have you ever had the experience of setting a goal, achieving it, and then after a brief "good" feeling, experiencing a letdown and a shrug of the shoulders that said, "Okay, what's next?" I certainly have. What I've learned is this might mean you set your goal for the wrong reason. A lack of long-term fulfillment from reaching a goal may indicate that it was an ego-based goal with a short-term fulfillment factor. To repeat a phrase mentioned in an earlier chapter, it may have been a goal that keeps you on the "hedonic treadmill."

One of the keys to happiness is to have a sense of accomplishment. It's important to make contributions to society either through your work or by volunteering. One way to ensure you are contributing at your highest level is to set goals and be accountable to them. Merely thinking about them isn't going to get you there. It doesn't always have to be some big accomplishment; it can be very small, and as you start to gain a little mastery, you can then move to another level.

Goals are the milepost markers along the road to happiness. Sometimes we aim for markers that are too close and the goals are 100 percent achievable. Other times, we aim for markers too far out and there's no chance we'll ever get there. When your goals are too achievable, you aren't stretching yourself enough. When a goal is unachievable, it's more of a dream. Many of us hear a lot about goals and spend plenty of time making lists of them, but we don't always think about them in terms of how achievable they are and how they can potentially help carry out our purpose.

One way to carry out your purpose is by setting financial goals. These goals can be some of the most important. If you're not presently a master of your cash flow, you might have to begin with making a budget. "Budget" is a dreaded word out there—it can be your taskmaster or accountability partner. There's a big difference. Budgets, and sometimes other goals, are often too confining. Rather than planning out where every penny is to be spent, try seeing where it all went. I have found that asking where it went might be more effective than saying I can only spend X amount per month. I like to approach budgeting by asking myself, *Am I being accountable for the money that's there?*

Hindsight perspective—for budgeting and other goals—is more refreshing and helps us see whether we're staying accountable to our purpose. Although you'd never drive a car looking only in your rear-view mirror, sometimes it can be helpful to glance in the mirror to see where you have been.

## ALIGNING GOALS

Early on in my marriage, my wife and I did what most newly married couples do—we worked to get a handle on where our money was going. I started recording in a pocket spiral notebook where I was spending money. Something became quite clear to me in this process—there was a lot of money being spent that I was unaware of. My original motive for detailed accounting was that I was convinced my wife was the budget spoiler. It was kind of uncomfortable to discover I was more responsible than I originally thought. Eventually, we came to a marital agreement that I wasn't allowed to go into technology stores alone anymore. I've since developed a little more restraint, but it's clearly my budget spoiler. My first responsibility was to be accountable. It did provide some insights to build on, and once I was able to do that, reaching other goals became a lot easier.

I've used many types of goal-setting methods to carry out my purpose—some have been financial and some personal development. A recent goal of mine has been to lose weight. It's one thing to have a doctor say to me that I should lose a little weight; I know that. But as soon as he says to me, "Do you want to be able to play basketball with your grandkids?" there's emotion tied to it. The goal is more motivating because it's aligned with my values. Again, I have to start small. I look to see whether I can improve just one aspect. It's certainly not easy, but it's another way for me to carry out my purpose and to keep it aligned with my H.E.A.R.T.

Aligning goals with my values has led to greater satisfaction. The goal can be a milepost for accomplishment, but it's not satisfying if it's not aligned with my values. When they align, I'm more motivated instead of feeling it's something I have to do. The key has been to have my goals be more satisfying by making sure they are part of my "why."

## THE DRIVING FORCE OF GOALS

I don't achieve every goal I set, but if I can stretch myself and still achieve at least 80 percent of them, that's great. The first step is to get clear about what you want and why you want it and then take positive action. You have to commit to it. Each goal is a stepping-stone to carry out your larger purpose. You don't need to lay the whole road map out to begin with; identify just one activity you're going to change and celebrate the process.

Goals challenge you. They stretch you to think bigger and try harder than you would without them. They help you measure your progress through life. When set for the right reasons, goals can motivate you to take action when you're tired, to dream big when you're feeling small, and to persevere when you face obstacles. The power of achieving goals is aligning your motives with your values.

This starts with making sure your goals are balanced. They should encompass the four elements of True Wealth and true happiness—physical, spiritual, emotional, and financial health. They should be short term and long term. They should be personal and professional, internal and external. You might ask yourself, *How do I want to grow spiritually? What do I want to do in the community? How do I improve my attitude?*

I often say this, and it comes from a Zig Ziglar quote: "Your attitude, not your aptitude, will determine your altitude."

## REACHING OUR MILEPOSTS

To avoid that feeling of letdown or a lack of long-term fulfillment from reaching a goal, I suggest that each time you set one, ask yourself, *Am I setting this goal for the right reasons? Is this goal congruent with my values, my personal mission statement, and what is best for me and those people most important to me?* If your answer is yes, then the world will conspire to help make those goals happen, and you'll be intrinsically satisfied when you achieve them. If your answer is no, you may still achieve the goal, but it may turn out to be a hollow victory.

There aren't many guarantees in life, but if you don't have a goal, you're guaranteed to achieve it. To help more of us be accountable through our goals, here are a few things to consider:

1. Make your goals 50/50. As you set your goals, set them so you believe in your heart of hearts there is a 50/50 chance of achieving them. If you achieve 90 to 100 percent of your goals, you are not stretching

yourself. Of course, a bigger goal might consist of several smaller mileposts. For your very first goal, you might want it to be 100 percent achievable, to gain a little momentum, but be sure to stretch yourself more each subsequent time. Many of us are overly familiar with setting goals, but many of us don't stop to think whether they're achievable *and* going to stretch us.

2. Make sure your goals meet the SMAC test. They need to be specific, measurable, achievable, and compatible with your values and purpose in life. Getting your goals right makes the journey easier on your way to True Wealth and happiness. For example, if your goal is to save two thousand dollars, that's specific and measurable, so you pass on the first two. To see whether it's achievable, it's a whole lot easier to break that down into how much that is per month or per day. Lastly, be sure it's compatible with your values and your purpose. How do you plan to use the two thousand dollars?

3. Create an action plan. Ask yourself these three questions: What's my goal in the next week, month,

year, five years? What actions do I need to take to achieve it? What's my reward? Maybe my goal is to hire an associate. What do I need to do? I need to post the job opening. What's my reward? My reward is having more time. When looking at rewards, look at long-term as well as intrinsic rewards.

Setting goals aligned with your values that carry out your purpose gives you a deeper and longer-term sense of fulfillment when accomplishing them. Whatever your goal, start small, gain mastery, and celebrate the journey. Be sure you aim for milepost markers on each road to your happiness—physical, spiritual, emotional, and financial—that aren't too easy to achieve or too far away to reach. When you have a big goal, break it down and work backward: *What do I have to do? Is the goal achievable? Is there an element of stretch? Is it aligned with my purpose?* This is how we can use our goals to further our mission in the world and lead more fulfilling and meaningful lives.

Chapter 6

# CHERISH
# RELATIONSHIPS

*"At the end of your life, you will never regret not having passed one more test, not winning one more verdict or not closing one more deal. You will regret time not spent with a husband, a friend, a child, or a parent."*

—Barbara Bush

## WHERE MEANING IS FOUND

When was the last time you spent quality time with someone important to you? With social media nowadays, it's nearly impossible not to have hundreds, if not thousands, of "friends." Yet having significant relationships is increasingly difficult in our society. We might be getting more social but not necessarily more meaningful. Don't get me wrong; I love Facebook and am fascinated by it, but I fear we're losing the ability to socialize and have core relationships with people we can truly call friends.

Nothing in life is more enriching than having close, genuine relationships with those you love. As we all know, relationships are not easy. They require attention, commitment, and a sincere desire to be close to another human being. If you miss out on true, heartfelt relationships, you will miss out on life itself. Research from the University of Chicago's National Opinion Research Center indicates that people with five or more close friends are 60 percent more likely to describe themselves as "very happy" compared to people who listed no close friends. These are not your Facebook or LinkedIn friends; these are intimate friends. Getting to share our journey with the people who matter most makes the road trip more meaningful.

Many of us know that relationships are good for us, but how many take the time to cherish them? A key lesson from the longest study on happiness is that it's the quality of relationships, not just having them, that matters (Waldinger 2015). This is why it doesn't really matter how many friends you have on Facebook. Are you spending time with them? Are you making memories with them? Are you there for them when they need you? It's important to feel like you can count on others when the going gets tough. Many of us are told that a relationship is supposed to be 50/50, but a wise pastor once told me that for a marriage to make it, it requires 100 percent effort. If both partners in the relationship spent 100 percent of their effort making sure the other person's needs were being met, they would discover both of them had their needs fulfilled. As I mentioned earlier, love isn't about how much we *get*; it's about how much we *give*. To have a relationship that's good for both parties, each person needs to give 100 percent.

Throughout the book, we've looked at finding more happiness by defining what matters most, living that out, and accomplishing our purpose through our goals, but none of that ultimately matters if there is no one around to share it with. In one of my favorite movies, *For the Love of the Game*, Billy Chapel, a legendary baseball player, is nearing the end of a magnificent career. Throughout the game, you see him reflect on his life, every pitch bringing him closer to the end of his career and the completion of a perfect game. After he wins, there's an initial celebration, but soon he finds himself back in his room alone, and he begins to sob. He ultimately seeks out the one person who really matters in his life but to whom he had been unable to commit. At this point he realizes why he felt empty instead of elated completing a perfect game. Without relationships, achieving things is often meaningless. The thing is, we often take relationships for granted and remember to cherish them only when it's too late.

## BEFORE IT'S TOO LATE

My life—and what it means to cherish relationships—took on a new meaning because of my relationship with my dad. He lived his life cherishing those who meant the most to him. Before he passed away, we had a few weeks to spend time with him and say all the things that had been implied or unspoken. Not everyone is this lucky.

My dad was a teacher and a pastor until the very end. The Friday night before he passed, we were standing around his bedside. He said to us, "It looks like we may have a funeral in the near future." His next words were, "I am ready if the funeral is mine; the important question is, are you ready if it happens to be yours?" Here is my dad, two breaths away from not being here, and he wants to make sure we're ready. That was a real gut-check moment. I'm grateful I had the chance to say the things I needed to say to my dad before he was gone. For some of us, expressing our feelings might not be who we are, kind of like how my dad wasn't a hugger for most of his life. In these cases, action is more powerful than the spoken word. Creating time to spend together is what matters.

This is what heading north and living a life of happiness based on True Wealth are about. The people I most valued in my life were with me at *Happiness*. If I think about my happiest life moments—my marriage to my wife over thirty-seven years ago, my children, spending time with my parents—they all point to the relationships I most cherish.

With the passing of my dad, I realized how easy it is to cherish relationships more when they are gone. Of course, I still cherish the memories and all the joy because they still remain, like a bobber hitting the water and creating a ripple; eventually the bobber gets pulled out, but you still feel and see its effect. This is why the other principles of True Wealth also matter. When we live a life of love based on our values, carry out our purpose through our goals, and share our lives with the people who matter most, we can create this ripple effect so we can cherish them long after they are gone.

## WHAT IT MEANS TO CHERISH

For me, to cherish means knowing a relationship can be gone in an instant and that it exists for a reason.

When you cherish relationships, you value them versus feeling they're an obligation. With all the evidence out there of how good relationships are for you, this should be a lot easier. Family and friends are vital to your happiness. The wider and deeper the relationships you have, the better (Rudin 2006).

It turns out that various kinds of social relationships, such as being married, having contact with friends, and being a member of a church or other organization, can help you live longer. The results of a study that covered nearly five thousand men and women indicated that for men and women across all age groups, those who were low or lacking in these types of relationships at the beginning of the study in 1965 were 30 to 300 percent more likely to have died during the subsequent years.

If you still need reasons to cherish relationships, studies have shown that the premature death rate for divorced, single, and widowed individuals is consistently higher than for married people (Ortmeye 1974). Now you understand why insurance companies want to know your marital status, because it's one of the best predictors of how long you're likely to live. Interestingly, the numbers show that marriage adds an average of seven years to the life of a man and about four to that of a woman (Rudin 2006). There's probably more behind the inequality of these numbers, but I think that's an issue best left for future writings.

I previously stated that money can't buy happiness, and research once again delivers proof. Apparently, friendships have a much greater effect on our overall happiness than our income does (Rudin 2006), one more reason to put relationships higher on your priority list. Another finding from the longest happiness study found that "[i]t was the capacity for intimate relationships that predicted flourishing in all aspects of these men's lives" (McKay and McKay 2014). It appears that when we cherish relationships, other areas of life become elevated.

## CREATING A RIPPLE EFFECT

So how do you create a ripple? How do you make sure your accomplishments and dreams have more meaning? Begin by setting aside space and time to nurture your relationships. This is what heading north provided me. Dad realized we needed to get away from our normal activities and spend time on relationships—quality time, not just hanging out together. But this space and time can happen anywhere.

I invite you to reflect back and identify relationships that mean the most to you. Start to cherish them or reconnect with them. It's important you have people with whom you can share your greatest struggles, anxieties, and deepest joys, whether it's your spouse, your kids, or whomever. It's so easy to take them for granted when you have the security of knowing they're there. The time to cherish them is now, not when they're gone. Here's a couple of ways you can start to do that:

1. Don't take a relationship for granted. Liven it up by doing something new together (taking long walks, going on date nights). This is a great way to avoid falling into a routine and taking your loved ones for granted. My wife would probably say I need to take a dose of my own medicine, which is why it's important to have these reminders.

2. Replace "screen time" with "people time." Many of us are familiar with this scene. You go out to dinner and see a table of people, all with their heads down over their devices waiting for the meal to arrive. They aren't engaging with each other. You might even be that table. Try putting the phone away during meals or even carving out "device-free" time throughout the day or week and practicing giving your presence instead.

By now you should understand that satisfying relationships can protect you when you go through the bumps, potholes, and detours on your road north. Not only is it good for our social life; social connection is also good for your health. Too often, you think you get a genuine social connection through your social media or spending an entire evening on your phones instead of engaging with one another. It seems you should not only be eating your sprouts and spinach if you want to live a long, healthy life; you should also be putting down your phone and connecting with your loved ones (Waldinger 2015).

Chapter 7

# VALUE YOUR HEALTH

*"He who has health, has hope; and he who has hope, has everything."*
—Thomas Carlyle

## THE COST OF RUNNING OUT OF GAS

A very dear friend once told me he spent the majority of his life building wealth. He realized he had not taken appropriate care of himself along the way and then found he was using most of his wealth in an effort to maintain his health. Dealing with ill health is often when we wish we had taken better care of ourselves.

Although the average person is living longer, studies show that more than one-third of our population is still dying prematurely from preventable causes, such as smoking, poor diet, physical inactivity, and alcohol consumption.

Research says that poor diet and physical inactivity may overtake tobacco as the leading cause of death (Mokdad et al 2004). Let's look at it a different way. If you had a million-dollar racehorse, would you feed it hamburgers, keep it up all night, give it alcohol, and expect it to compete? Probably not. You would treat a horse of that caliber with a precise diet and training. So why don't we take better care of our bodies? Changing your behavior might add years to your life and save money on health care and prescription drugs (Raymond 2016).

We spend massive amounts of money to extend our lives, and rightly so if our goal is not to die early. Leading health expert John Robbins, author of *Healthy at 100*, says that in the past one hundred years, we have added about thirty years to the average life expectancy of people in the industrialized world. He goes on to say that one hundred years ago, the average adult in Western nations spent only 1 percent of his or her life in a morbid or ill state but today's average, modern adult spends more than 10 percent of his or her life being sick. He says people are *living* longer today, but all too often, they are *dying* longer, too. Some people have increased their life spans but not necessarily their health spans.

Do you remember the exercise of picturing what your life would be like if you were financially confident, physically fit, spiritually nourished, and surrounded by loving relationships? The journey toward True Wealth is not all about money and requires balance. The irony is that your financial resources, although they appear to be their own category, represent the one area that is woven throughout all areas of life. If you're missing work because you're not healthy, there's a financial effect. If you're not able to save because you're paying medical bills, there's a financial effect. Research has also found an association between weight loss and wealth accumulation. Findings show that "some people develop a 'prevention mindset' where they are likely to consider the future implications of present-day activities such as reading nutrition labels and saving money" ("The Financial Impact of Improved Health Behaviors" 2016).

Maintaining good health practices is one of my greatest personal struggles. Life is busy, and if something has to fall by the wayside, frequently it's taking care of my physical body. In fact, the number-one reason people say they don't exercise is lack of time. I do value my health more than I used to because as I get older, I have a greater sense of mortality. Recently, I bent over to tie my shoes and was amazed at being out of breath. When did that happen? It's amazing how fast you can get out of shape.

## THE BALANCE BETWEEN
## SURVIVAL AND EXCESS

If you were to take a look at my body fat results, you might wonder whether I had even read this chapter. This is definitely the principle I most need to work on.

It's a constant struggle for me. Growing up, if it was on the table and wasn't moving, it was fair game for your fork. You can imagine that I developed some bad habits. I told my doctor that maybe if I eat fast enough, I can get my heart rate up high enough to burn the extra calories. He didn't seem to buy it. So then I tried to appease him by saying I run to the refrigerator each day. He said that would be fine if the refrigerator were fifteen miles away. I've always admired people with the 26.2 stickers on their cars—running has never been something I've enjoyed. I have a treadmill in my basement, and the only time I get any exercise is when I'm cleaning and have to move it.

My enjoyment of food didn't come from a stranger. I remember my dad talking about a time his doctor told him he needed to cut back on bacon. He said, "But I like it, so why should I consider such a change?" The doctor told him it could potentially add five years to his life. Dad's response was "But I have been witness to a lot of people's last five years, and they aren't their best five." I believe they came to an agreement about balance and moderation. I wonder if that's why he would often have sausage—for the sake of balance. Your health is important, and what you put into your body matters, but I also find it interesting how many people who have longevity occasionally bent almost all the rules. So heredity has some influence, but we still have an effect on our overall health.

Warren Buffet, one of the most successful investors in the world, told shareholders at a recent Berkshire Hathaway meeting in Omaha that he drinks around seven hundred calories' worth of Coca-Cola a day. He said, "I am doing the things I enjoy." You have to know the things you like. He said he often wished he had a twin so the twin would eat only broccoli. He said it's possible his twin might be healthier, but he was sure he would not be as happy. He also stated that he knows what his total caloric intake should be for the day but that he chooses to get a certain amount of his calories from the things he likes and then makes sure the remaining calories come from healthier choices. He does what makes him happy while trying to maintain a balance.

I know my health is important, but I struggle to maintain it. It's a constant balance between survival and excess. When other areas of my life are off course, my health suffers the most because it's my weakest point. Whatever area tends to be our weakest might be where we lose sight first when other things are out of balance. It's not easy trying to keep all areas in balance, and it takes work. At times it can be a little like herding cats.

## WHERE ALL ROADS CONVERGE

This is where it all comes together. Health and True Wealth are related in many ways. Being healthy positively contributes to your relationships, financial wealth, and ability to carry out your purpose and achieve your goals. Equally, being happy, having positive emotions and lots of close friends, and being in loving relationships all contribute to your health. The flipside is also true. When any of these areas are off course, your health suffers. The ancient philosopher Virgil was once quoted as saying, "The greatest wealth is health." My philosophy is that being healthy leads to more wealth, and I'm not just talking about monetary wealth. So exercising and eating right are in our best interest.

I like to think of health as a three-legged stool. Healthy eating is the first leg. What you put into your body is fuel, and the better fuel you use, the more efficiently you'll run. Putting the wrong fuel in your body could lead to lethargy, obesity, and all kinds of health problems. As I mentioned, my enjoyment of food makes this one of my greatest personal struggles. Putting a set goal into writing provides me an additional number of accountability partners to encourage me and help me strive to improve this important area of True Wealth.

Aerobic exercise is the second leg. It offers several benefits, including a stronger heart, weight loss, and the release of endorphins. Endorphins are "happy" chemicals released by the brain. They help you feel euphoric and reduce stress and anxiety. Being aerobically fit also boosts your immune system, so you'll be less susceptible to minor colds and the flu.

Strength training is the third leg. After about age thirty-five, we lose roughly half a pound of muscle a year. Diet and aerobic exercise are important, but if that's all you do, you'll end up thin and weak. Strength training will keep your muscles active and growing and help keep your fat down.

The bottom line is, the better shape you're in, the better you'll feel and the more you'll be able to do and enjoy life. I believe I was created by a Creator, which means I have a responsibility to take care of my physical body.

## DRIVING A WELL-OILED MACHINE

Now, I can talk to you until I'm blue in the face about the benefits of exercising, but the truth is that giving you facts will not change your behavior. What can change your behavior is emotion. For you to exercise more, you have to come up with a compelling reason that makes the benefits of exercising outweigh the initial pain and what some proclaim is a hassle. Rather than trying to scare yourself into getting in better shape, look for ways that being healthier can bring more joy into your life. I know what I'm supposed to do, but that knowledge by itself doesn't get me exercising. But when my doctor asked whether I planned on playing basketball with my grandchildren the way I did with my children, that emotional reason provided additional motivation. It doesn't guarantee success, but it does increase the probability of an effort to improve.

Start with knowing what "health" means to you. Once you know your values, then you have emotion connected to your goals, which gives you more motivation. Remember, your physical health is one component of True Wealth, and the key is to find balance. I'm not saying it's more or less important than the other areas, but if you're not feeling well, that's not balance, which will affect everything else. It's important to learn how not to take your health for granted, but we each have to find our own path. Here are a few suggestions on how to get started:

1. Identify what makes you happy. Find things that work, and get your foothold there. The tricky thing is it's a balance between survival (we have to eat

and keep our bodies healthy) and enjoyment (we are here to enjoy life and all True Wealth has to offer us). Much like Dad with bacon and Warren Buffet with Coca-Cola, find those things you enjoy and where you can trade them for other things.

2. Lay out a plan for how you want to improve. Once you know what matters most, set your health goals based on that and attach an emotional reason to getting healthy. Know what "health" means to you and why you value it. Then set your compass and find an accountability partner to help you stay focused on reaching your milepost markers along the way.

3. Seek out other counsel. Look for people who are professionals in the area where you are the weakest, and admit you may need help in this area—just like hiring a financial adviser to get your financial health in balance. If you have a relationship accountability partner, all the better, but perhaps you need a trainer to keep yourself accountable. Paying someone might increase the probability you'll go see him or her. It's also important to recognize how your financial resources are continually woven throughout every area of your life.

The key here is to value your health and see it as integral to your overall True Wealth. Then take the necessary steps, which requires all areas of the three-legged stool for balance. Right now, I'm zero for three, so I personally admit the need to improve. I realize that until this is in place, I won't be able to grow in other areas. Even though it's a struggle, trying is better than giving up.

Chapter 8

# WISELY USE
# YOUR FINANCIAL
# RESOURCES

*"People tend to treat their finances like their dentistry. They assume the man handling it knows what he is doing."*

—Dick Cavett

## VEERING OFF COURSE

We all know how hard it is to earn money, so the last thing we want to do is spend it frivolously, right? Well, unfortunately, there are many people in our country who do not wisely use their financial resources. If a stranger got his hands on your bank or credit card statement, how would you feel? Would you be embarrassed? Would it show foolish spending and indulgence? Would it show you are a good steward with a generous heart?

There's a scene in *Finding Nemo* where the seagulls come in and annoyingly call "Mine, mine, mine, mine." It's kind of funny in a movie script, but in managing finances, not so much. My resources are not all "mine"; I have a certain responsibility to manage them for myself, for my relationships, and for the betterment of society as a whole.

Sometimes money can be what moves us off course. Many of us think that if we just had more money, then we could do so many other things. Money is a tool for carrying out our values, living our purpose, being healthy, and living a life of love, but if we forget about these things, happiness can be elusive. It's not about wasting money or seeing it as the be all, end all; it's about being able to take control of your financial resources instead of their taking control of you.

Some see money as the root of all evil (which needs to be clarified because the quote is actually "the *love of money is the root of all evil*"). Some people see having money as the only way to enjoy life. One of our exercises in the Five Blueprinting Steps to True Wealth is to complete several sentences. Here are two examples:

- "Money is ..."
- "If I had all the money I need, I would ..."

How would you complete those two sentences? Remember, money can be your greatest ally or your greatest enemy.

Many of us are trained from an early age to spend, to treat ourselves. When I was a child, there was a popular fast-food burger chain with a marketing campaign aimed at reminding us "You deserve a break today." When it comes to managing our financial resources, statistics suggest that the average American spends approximately one-and-a-half times more than he or she earns through the use of credit cards. Even the plastic we carry is misleading. Unless you are drawing from an account with assets in it (which would be a debit card), the company extends you credit. So what you have when you use the card is debt. If you thought of it as a debt card, you might hesitate before pulling the plastic from your wallet. Managing your financial resources can be as simple as never spending more than you make. Unfortunately, in today's society, we are all on a quest for more, so the battle continues.

## STRIKING A BALANCE

As a part of my responsibilities when I was a deacon at the church, I was making visitations to a couple of individuals at a long-term care facility. One of them had a significant net worth; the other did not. When I was visiting with the elderly man who had been very successful and accumulated sizeable financial resources, he said something very intriguing: "I spent most of my life trying to accumulate and protect my wealth. Now I look around and the only distinguishing difference between most of us is the color of our rooms."

He was reflecting on his life, saw that money was what drove everything for him, and wondered whether he had wisely used it. He found himself at a point in time when the money didn't really make a difference.

My dad always said, "If I have cash flow coming in beyond my expenses and I have enough to help organizations, ministries, or missions that match my passions and I can do what I want, I am a wealthy man." This was my dad's view on financial security. He taught me what it meant to be a "steward"—how we're taking care of it on behalf of somebody else. My dad had a deep understanding of being a financial steward. He knew as long as he was spending his money on the things that were important and aligned with his principles, he was wisely using his financial resources.

## DEEPENING YOUR RELATIONSHIP
## WITH MONEY

Financial resources are the central thread that weaves through every area of True Wealth, but if they are all we focus on, we end up with assets and no meaning. People who focus only on money come up short. People who focus only on the other areas and not money can't do what they want to do. To give takes money. To improve your health takes money. To improve your education takes money. To clothe, feed, and educate your children takes money. Bottom line—they all take money!

So how are we to manage our finances wisely? By approaching them as a financial steward. Think of managing your finances as being a steward on a ship. The steward takes care of your luggage to make sure it gets where it needs to, safely and on time. The same thing goes for financial resources. If you believe they are gifts from God and entrusted to you or you see them as needing to be aligned with what matters most, you'll treat them differently. Your relationship with money deepens when you identify its purpose.

Generally, when you meet people who are wise financial stewards, they don't have as much anxiety. They typically have it figured out. They've identified where funds should go and are looking at the long term.

They're committed to a plan and a process. Unfortunately, many people are a paycheck or two away from a financial tragedy. The people who have mastered the wise management of their financial resources have a sense of calm. Even when huge tragedies come, they are better prepared and have potentially less worry.

## HOW TO INSTILL CONFIDENCE
## ABOUT MONEY

It's easy enough to worry about finances. I'd say this is probably the number-one thing most people worry about. It's certainly a cause of distress in most relationships, but the way I see it, there are different types of worry. There's the "what if something comes up?" worry, which is because you don't have enough in savings—you're afraid of running out of gas. If you are worrying about the long term, that means you haven't identified what matters most and what you need to do to get there—you're afraid of getting lost. I like to keep my worrying to those things I can control. Do I have a road map? Am I sticking to it and saving appropriately? Am I checking in on it? There's no point in worrying about the things I can't control. There'll always be unexpected surprises with various effects. Here's where we can go back to what we can control—having something extra set aside.

Think of building financial wealth a little at a time. There are really only three ways to legally manage your financial obligations and help grow your financial wealth: work for your money, let your money work for you, or receive charity (other people work to provide you money). Focus on having a career that aligns with your core values and getting paid to do those services. Then think of how to effectively manage those resources for the accomplishment of specific goals or charitable opportunities that help you carry out your purpose. Here are a few other things to consider when using your resources wisely:

1. Pay yourself first. Most of us do the opposite and pay ourselves last. Dedicate some of the funds before they all get allocated. We often say we'll pay

ourselves from what's left, but all the money's usually gone by the time we get around to it. It's important to put something aside for the detours along the way. This way, when an emergency comes up, you don't have to worry.

2. Know where you're going. Having more confidence about money is identifying what your objectives, goals, and timeframe are and setting up an action plan to carry those things out. Saving and investing appropriately are important, but they need to have a purpose. You can lay out the most beautiful financial road map, but if it doesn't align with what's important to you, you won't do it. Your goals need to have motivation behind them, just like working out or any other goals you set for yourself.

3. Identify your passions. Complete this sentence: "If money were no issue, I would ..." The answer provides some clarity as to what the purpose of money is in your life. It can also give you some insight into your relationship with money. This leads nicely into the next principle regarding what you might be passionate about or where you might

want to be philanthropic. You've got to connect your money to your purpose to know you're pursuing more for the right reasons.

Here's a checklist to gain some additional perspective on what you feel and believe about money:

- ✓ Are you paying yourself first?
- ✓ Are you taking advantage of tax-favored investments?
- ✓ Are you avoiding frivolous impulse spending?
- ✓ Are you living within your means?
- ✓ Are your long-term financial commitments in harmony with your long-term family goals and your values?

Wisely using your financial resources means avoiding impulse spending, living within your means, and setting a little extra aside. These are all sound principles, but nothing new or profound. Take a few moments to sit down—and if there is a spouse or significant other, do this together—and go through your last bank or credit card statement. Are there any things that, in hindsight, you wish had not consumed part of your financial resources? Are there any patterns in your spending that look out of line? Going through this type of exercise might be the spark that causes you to make changes in how you use your financial resources—like a frivolous seagull or a wise steward.

Chapter 9

# BE COMPASSIONATE
# WITH THE WORLD

*"If you want others to be happy,*
*practice compassion. If you want*
*to be happy, practice compassion."*

—Dalai Lama

## GIVING UNTIL IT FEELS GOOD

Compassion is certainly something we could use more of in this world. We don't have to look very far to see suffering. Sometimes we might find ourselves saying, "Okay, I was compassionate with the world." Check, move on. Though it can be easy to be compassionate with our loved ones, it can be a completely different story with those we do not know, unless we have had a similar experience. Going through difficult times gives us greater perspective. It awakens our sensitivities and helps us identify with others. There's not a single person who hasn't been down a difficult road.

None of us lives an isolated life. In his famous poem, John Donne said, "No man is an island, / Entire of itself, / Every man is a piece of the continent, / A part of the main." Yes, our very existence depends on the help of others. Once we realize how much we all need each other, it becomes easier to develop a sense of universal altruism. I know this sounds a little Pollyanna-ish, but by making a little extra effort to help relieve the suffering in the world, we can all make the world a better place.

One way to be more compassionate is to give, to share more of our financial resources with those in need. Yet often when we think of giving in this way, most people think of the tax benefit or quid pro quo. Certainly, there is still good that can come from this, but it's much more fulfilling when we identify what we're passionate about and how to be compassionate with the world with no strings attached. I find the most inspirational example of compassion to be when someone asks, "Who funded this?" and I don't know because there was no name attached. That's truly giving without strings.

Someone told me one time that instead of giving until it hurts, give until it feels good. That's true; giving makes us feel good. It turns out that there's another benefit of giving. Recent studies have shown that people who give more actually grow richer. That seems a little counterintuitive, doesn't it? If you give away your money, you'd think you'd end up with less, not more, but that's not necessarily what happens. When being compassionate is an extension of living a life based on True Wealth, it's a higher level of compassion. Usually, when you give to others, you think you're improving their lives—which you are—but the real benefit comes back to you. Not only are you humbled by thinking *Wow, that could happen to me*, but you also experience an unexplainable benefit.

People who are charitable tend to get promoted into positions of leadership, which leads to higher income. As other people notice your charitable convictions, more opportunities tend to come your way, and that can lead to higher income. Please understand that I'm not suggesting that you buy into the "prosperity gospel" that many people promote as a spiritual strategy to get wealthy. I would encourage you to give more because it is aligned with your H.E.A.R.T. and you have a sincere desire to embrace your passions and better those around you.

Science tells us that freely giving stimulates the parts of the brain that are associated with meeting our basic needs. Could it be that part of our basic nature is to want to give, reach out, and be compassionate? That's a nice thought. This is where it helps to see money as a tool but not as the only means. Unfortunately, much of the time, money is connected to greed. Giving with no strings attached from a place of compassion is the opposite of that. That's why it's important first to identify those things directly aligned with you and your values that you can contribute to "with passion."

There are plenty of times when we overlook people who are in need right in our backyards. We can start small in specific targeted areas that are right at home.

## TRUE COMPASSION

By now, you should know this is a self-help book, and just as with many of these principles, this is also an area on which I continually need to focus. In 2014, while my parents were up north, their home, along with many others, was damaged by the flood that hit northwest Iowa. The water in the basement was two inches away from the ceiling tile. I couldn't believe the number of people who showed up to help. People in a line of pickups and an old-fashioned fire brigade emptied everything out of the main floor in amazing time. Many larger items were rescued from the basement before the Rock River levee broke. The number of people who showed up to help clean out the dirty water still amazes me. There was a local resident I knew growing up who was there at the break of dawn, pushing around the dirtiest water imaginable, all the while whistling or singing top-ten country songs. I remember thinking, *These are my parents; I have to be here. But why is he here?* Later on in the day, we were all covered in mud, and this guy was joking around and having a great time. Once again I found myself thinking, *Man, I'd really like to be home right now; this is terrible.* I finally said to him, "I'm just curious. I'm here out of obligation; why are you here?" He said, "I experienced a similar situation a few years ago. I had a flood and had no clue where to even begin, and out of the blue, twenty-five people showed up and helped me fix it."

Here I was thinking I had showed up to be compassionate, but he was truly compassionate. There's a difference. This man did it out of love, out of servitude. He was obviously living a life of True Wealth. That was an incredibly humbling experience.

I had a mentor and a father who went to visit the sick. It was part of his position, but he was in his position because he was passionate about it. Though serving others was a natural extension of his work, it was also a natural extension of his living a life based on True Wealth. He found serving others to be fulfilling because it aligned with what mattered most to him.

## SHARING OUR TRUE WEALTH
## WITH OTHERS

When you achieve True Wealth, you think beyond yourself and want to share it with others. This is the point of living out these principles. At first it is introspective, but when you start looking beyond that, you become more energized by saying, "I want to share this with people; I want more people to experience this."

Compassion is when we feel sympathy for someone in distress and then strive to eliminate or lessen it. It can be hard to do this if we don't have some form of spirituality, we aren't mentally engaged, our finances aren't in order, or our physical health is suffering. Being compassionate is an extension of True Wealth and is the most natural next step and one of the most gratifying. It's the final milepost marker on your journey to happiness. You don't do it so you can say you're there; you're there so you can do it.

I really like how St. Francis described it. He said, "Where you see despair, bring hope; where you see darkness, bring light; where you see sadness, bring joy." I don't think there's one item in the world we need to be compassionate about; I think there are many. There are certain things you'll give more freely to than others. They're all equally important. Notice that inside the word "compassion" is "passion." The goal is to find what things you're most inspired by and you think need to be changed and then have compassion for those passions and do your best to make the world a better place. The road north is far more fulfilling when you take this approach.

## FINDING THE PASSION IN COMPASSION

I invite you to sit down and answer this question: "If I could make a difference in the world, what would it be?" It's good to identify those things and give to those areas. If you can give financially, that certainly helps, but it takes more than just money to be compassionate. If you're just starting out, you can integrate giving of your financial resources along the way. Serving others at a homeless shelter, organizing a group to feed hungry kids, or giving of your time are other ways to be compassionate that are invaluable.

What items are at the top of your passion list? What are you inspired by? How can you help? Some of these things aren't always comfortable. They can take us out of our comfort zones. Here are a few other suggestions to help you determine the kind of difference you might want to make in the world:

1. Identify your pet cause. If you were going to write an editorial to your local newspaper on an issue you felt strongly about, what issue would you choose? Why is that issue important to you?

2. Identify how you want to help. Given a choice, do you prefer to help people by rolling up your sleeves

and pitching in, or do you prefer to be a behind-the-scenes person? Think of three types of activities you would do to help people.

3. Pay it forward. When someone does that to me, I always think, *Oh, I should do that more often.* This is an example of giving with no strings attached. Plus, it fuels others and helps remind them to do more things like that. Find a way to pay it forward in your life and watch the effect it has.

When finding ways to be compassionate becomes a heartfelt thing—a natural extension of living a life based on True Wealth—opportunities are brought to your presence when you're least aware of them. Sometimes it's the smallest gesture that creates a domino effect. You might think you're changing one person's life, but much like a bobber hitting the water, the ripple effect is much larger than that.

Chapter 10

# BE OPEN TO WISE
# COUNSELORS

*"The next best thing to being wise oneself is to live in a circle of those who are."*

—C. S. Lewis

## LEARNING FROM OUR EXPERIENCES

Aristotle said that knowing yourself is the beginning of all wisdom. How do you get to know yourself? Through your experiences. Sometimes we think that if we can teach others about our experiences, we will keep them from making the same mistakes we did. Conceptually, that makes sense, but it's not always the best way to learn something. Often, I think back to something as simple as growing up having a gas stove. When the gas stove is off, it doesn't look hot anymore. My mom said, "Don't touch that; you'll get burned." But it didn't look hot anymore, so I touched it, an instant life lesson that provided wisdom. It's the same way for the more sophisticated and integral pieces of life.

For those of you who are parents, I'm sure you can relate to this. We give our kids guidance all the time based on our years of experience, but by golly, our kids don't always take our advice. The hard part is to try not to fix it all the time for them. Sometimes you have to let them go through those experiences first-hand. I think back on my life, and until I was about sixteen years old, my parents were incredibly wise. From about sixteen to twenty, all of a sudden, my parents lost all their marbles, but then I can remember a point in time after my wife and I got married when my parents got smart again. Going through it with my own kids now, I see that my parents didn't lose any wisdom over the years; I simply didn't respect their experiences as much during that period of time. I'm learning this is a process we all have to go through, though it sure would be a lot easier just to skip those teenage years!

I've seen great wisdom develop when I've told someone they should do something a certain way and then they don't. It wasn't an I-told-you-so moment; it was something they had to go through. They gained valuable knowledge and were able to apply that knowledge to make changes and get back on track. When you look at people who've become incredibly successful, they didn't always take the road straight north. One of the most successful storeowners I personally know first went bankrupt six or seven times before reaching success. As Edison so memorably said, "I have not failed. I've just found 10,000 ways that won't work."

Sometimes when traveling, you may need to stop to ask for directions on the road north. Equally, there are other times when you just need to take a wrong turn, learn from your mistakes, and find your way back to the main road. It takes a certain level of humility to be open to wise counsel, but that's how you grow and reach your destination. Sometimes counsel—whether from others or from your mistakes—comes to us in the most unexpected ways.

## UNEXPECTED COUNSELORS

When I was first starting out in the financial sector, I thought I had all the answers, and I was determined to teach my kids about the sound principles I was learning. My oldest son, Jon, was about five years old at the time. We talked about things like budgeting and tithing. I'd laid this all out and given him tasks so he could earn some money. I taught him to put some away for savings and some away for giving. I'd stressed to him that tithing, an Old Testament principle, was 10 percent. The New Testament principle teaches us to give as we have been blessed.

One day at church, the donation plate came around. Jon put in a dollar, and then I put in a dollar. I didn't think much of it because we had recently given in other areas. I hadn't noticed that he was watching, when he leaned over to me and said, "Dad, did you have a slow week?" I was crushed and speechless. He was looking to see whether I was carrying out what I was trying to teach him. Wise counsel can come from anywhere.

The moral for me is that no matter where it comes from or how much I've achieved or attained, there's always wise counsel to receive. Although I'm committed to living a life based on True Wealth and teaching these principles, it's important for me to regularly seek out others for reminders or to help me refocus. Sometimes we are a bit blind to our own experiences. This is when being open to wise counsel really comes in handy.

## WHAT IT MEANS TO BE WISE

Notice how this principle is about *being open to* wise counselors, not about *blindly following* wise counselors. I do not recommend that you blindly follow anyone. Instead, seek out others who can give you guidance, and then run it through your own filter. Your chances of being successful, by however you define success, will be greatly enhanced by seeking the advice of other experts. Learn what you can from them, filter it through your own understanding, and then move forward with action.

There's a difference between "book smart" and practical wisdom. Practical wisdom, Aristotle tells us, is "the combination of moral will and moral skill." Basically, it's knowing the right thing to do at the right time for the right reasons. It goes beyond rules and incentives. It's something you learn from life experiences and wise teachers. Life gives you those teaching moments, and people who are "wise" often have more life experiences. To seek out all forms of wisdom, especially from those who have experienced it, is important.

When looking for wise counsel, I'd suggest looking for someone with both knowledge and experience. There are certainly people who are in the profession of offering advice. Knowledge is the successful retention and understanding of data and facts. Wisdom is found, when through life's trials, we apply our experience to knowledge. Life is short, and age seems to accelerate time. Life comes at us quickly, so it's smart to surround

What wise counsel does this young peasant offer you? What can you learn from his tragic story and apply to your life? Being open to wise counsel means learning from our experiences and from the experiences of others. Wisdom is how we apply what we learn.

My hope is that this entire book has been an opportunity to practice being open to wise counsel. Living a life of True Wealth invites us to share what we have learned through our experiences and to continue learning from the experiences of others.

# CONCLUSION: FINDING YOUR ROAD NORTH

*"When all is said and done, our life will not be measured by what we have done but by the people we have touched."*

—Todd Linaman and Laura Sowers

The more you can incorporate these principles into your daily life, the more likely you'll be able to look back at the end of your life and have fewer regrets. A simple definition of a life well lived would be to say you have no sadness over what you might have done, might have been, or might have become. I think that's a worthy goal for everyone. Because you've taken the time to read this book, you still have time to make sure you'll have reached your destination on your road north.

True Wealth—true happiness—is the fruit of having all these areas we've talked about in sync and in balance. This is the road I'm trying to walk, and I invite you to join me on the journey. I invite you to make the True Wealth commitment. The commitment asks you to identify what you commit to having in your life, doing in your life, and being in your life.

When you think about it, as we mature through life, many of us follow the "having, doing, being" continuum. We start out wanting to have all kinds of material things in our lives. Then we realize all those things haven't brought us lasting happiness, so we decide we want to start doing things. This tends to happen around midlife and could manifest itself in the form of a midlife crisis. Once that passes, we move into the being stage. Here, we just want to be happy. We want to be in nature. We want to appreciate the simple things in life and find great joy in all we have that money can't buy and death can't take away.

Here are three final thoughts. First, happiness isn't a once-in-a-lifetime experience; it's something you can drive to each and every day. Happiness can be in your backyard; it's simply something you need to focus on, and it's about relationships and love. Material success comes and goes, but having a positive effect on people will echo across eternity.

Second, beginning your journey north to uncover true happiness may seem daunting. It requires you to be honest with yourself and to take a critical look within to uncover your deepest hopes, dreams, and aspirations. You may discover that you need to make major changes in your life, or you may discover that you've been on the right road all along and this just gives you confirmation of what you already know. The risk you take by not beginning your journey is that at the end of your days, you may look back on your life with regret. So step out of your comfort zone and begin your journey. Third, remember the Nine Principles of True Wealth:

1. Live a Life of Love
2. Stick to Your Core Values
3. Be Purpose Driven
4. Be Accountable through Your Goals

5. Cherish Relationships
6. Value Your Health
7. Wisely Use Your Financial Resources
8. Be Compassionate with the World
9. Be Open to Wise Counselors

Here are three additional resources to help you navigate your journey on *The Road North: Finding Happiness in True Wealth.*

1. You can request our Five Blueprinting Steps brochure, which will walk you through:
   a. Step One: Define What is Important to You
   b. Step Two: Discover Your Meaningful Purpose
   c. Step Three: Design a Compelling Vision for Your Future
   d. Step Four: Develop a Personal Mission Statement
   e. Step Five: Dedicate to Your Goals and Create an Action Plan
2. You can attend our individual or couples True Wealth Workshops.
3. You can subscribe to our True Wealth Podcast.

# BIBLIOGRAPHY

Gregoire, Carolyn. "The 75-Year Study That Found the Secrets to a Fulfilling Life." *The Huffington Post.* August 23, 2013. http://www.huffingtonpost.com/2013/08/11/how-this-harvard-psycholo_n_3727229.html.

Layard, Richard. *Happiness: Lessons from a New Science.* London: Penguin Books, 2006.

McKay, Brett and Kate McKay. "Love Is All You Need: Insights from the Longest Longitudinal Study on Men Ever Conducted." *The Art of Manliness.* September 2, 2014. http://www.artofmanliness.com/2014/09/02/love-is-all-you-need-insights-from-the-longest-longitudinal-study-on-men-ever-conducted/.

Mokdad, Ali H., James S. Marks, Donna F. Stroup, and Julie L. Gerberding. "Actual Causes of Death in the United States,

2000." *The JAMA Network.* March 10, 2004. http://jama.jamanetwork.com/article.aspx?articleid=198357.

Nuff, Kelly. "11 Ways to Live a Happier Life, According to a Psychologist (Hint: These Have Nothing to Do with Money!)." *The Mind Unleashed.* July 26, 2014. http://themindunleashed.org/2014/07/11-ways-live-happier-life-according-psychologist-hint-nothing-money.html.

Ortmeyer, C. F. "Variations in Mortality, Morbidity, and Health Care by Marital Status." In *Mortality and Morbidity in the United States,* edited by Carl L. Erhardt and Joyce E. Berlin, 159–84. Cambridge, MA: Harvard University Press, 1974.

Raymond, Chris. "The Top 10 Causes of Death in the United States." *VeryWell.* March 28, 2016. https://www.verywell.com/the-top-10-causes-of-death-in-the-united-states-1132450.

Rudin, Mike. "The Science of Happiness." *BBC News.* April 30, 2006. http://news.bbc.co.uk/2/hi/programmes/happiness_formula/4783836.stm.

Schwartz, Barry. "Barry Schwartz: Our Loss of Wisdom." *YouTube.* February 16, 2009. https://www.youtube.com/watch?v=1A-zdh_bQBo.

"The Financial Impact of Improved Health Behaviors." *Rutgers*. July 16, 2016. https://njaes.rutgers.edu/health finance/health-behaviors.asp.

Tolstoy, Leo. *How Much Land Does a Man Need?* Russia: Unknown, 1886.

Waldinger, Robert. "What Makes a Good Life? Lessons from the Longest Study on Happiness." *TED*. November 1, 2015. https://www.ted.com/talks/robert_waldinger_what_makes_a_good_life_lessons_from_the_longest_study_on_happiness?language=en#t-189606.

"What Is the Science of Happiness?" *Berkeley Wellness*. November 9, 2015. http://www.berkeleywellness.com/healthy-mind/mind-body/article/what-science-happiness.

"What Is Happiness?" *Greater Good*. June/July 2016. http://greatergood.berkeley.edu/topic/happiness/definition.

# ABOUT THE AUTHOR

Kevin is one of the region's first graduates from the True Wealth Institute in Omaha, Nebraska, as a True Wealth Consultant. Kevin brings an inspirational twist to financial and life planning. He believes that true wealth is defined as everything you have that money can't buy and death can't take away. The True Wealth Institute helps wealth advisers guide their relationships to works to discover and uncover *their own true wealth*, define what's important to them, and create a financial plan to work toward their individual financial goals.

**Kevin Engbers, CFP®**
*Wealth Advisor*
605.271.6023
kevin@PinnacleWealth
Management.com

- A CERTIFIED FINANCIAL PLANNER™ Practitioner since 1998
- Financial Planning Association Member
- *True Wealth* consultant

A native of Iowa, Kevin's blueprinting process provides a refreshing difference in helping people seek a balance in life. He is focused on simplifying the complex. In the financial services industry since 1987, he provides written comprehensive financial plans for people regardless of net worth to establish a foundation for financial planning. With a plan based on what is important to them, people are in a better position to live their lives with accountability and purpose.

Kevin and his wife, Linda, have been married since 1979 and have four sons. When not at the office, Kevin enjoys family time, especially loving (and spoiling) his grandchildren. He also enjoys yard work, boating, basketball, Big 10 sports (Go Hawkeyes!) and indulging in international cuisine.

**Kevin's Philosophy:**

Be driven by your purpose. Stick to your core values. Be accountable through your goals, cherish relationships, value health, find ways to be compassionate with the world, and be open to wise counselors.

612 E. Tan Tara Circle
Suite 100
Sioux Falls, SD 57108
www.PinnacleWealth.com
info@pinnaclewealth.com

Phone: 605.271.6023
Fax: 605.271.6032
Toll Free: 866.575.2500

Securities offered through Cetera Advisor Networks LLC, Member FINRA/SIPC. Investment advisory services offered through CWM, LLC, an SEC Registered Investment Advisor. Cetera Advisor Networks LLC is under separate ownership from any other named entity. Carson Group Partners, a division of CWM, LLC, is a nationwide partnership of advisors.